Ashes & Embers

for Spirit

Southern Reflections

Summer Blizzard

―――――― ∞ ――――――

On a bright afternoon
in Madison County, Georgia
a blizzard of cotton
blew from the bed
of a rusty truck
across a sizzling
black ribbon road.
Stopping
to gather the
raw softness
in her hand,
the stories
of Africans
came to her and she
was moved to
remember them.

Virginia Reel

———— ∞ ————

For Spirit, for M. & K.

Never did four hours pass
as close as last night's.
Was it a dream or a sudden madness between artists…
a Georgia man of French decent
and an honorary Southerner with a Yankee twist?
A bond of souls flashed underneath:
stalking, searing animal instincts.
The smell of liquor lingered under a silver orb.
The woods beckoned carelessly though
backward slants of time and place
caressed a feverish brow
laced with lemon verbena, southern sabers,
a rebel yell above cannon fire.

Theater On The Square

———— ∞ ————

They told you what art is and you didn't listen.
You took your clothes off.
You muttered profanity.
You mentioned homosexuality.
They told you what funding is and you didn't listen.
You cut back productions.
You threw out Actor's Equity.
You sold the complimentary seats.
They told you to conform and you didn't listen.
You packed up the technicians.
You put away the props.
You moved to another part of town.

Flea Market Fever

——— ∞ ———

St. Augustine women
come to the marketplace
to buy a lamp or
pretty picture
for a cluttered living room.
Cracked hands grasp
a dry flower in a
dusty vase and
a vial for Holy Water.
The women find a tin filled with buttons
lost or torn from
suits and dresses,
a Civil War tintype,
and an Indian arrowhead
resting on the table
beneath a shade tree.
Pieces from past lives
travel home in brown paper sacks.
They belong to the buyer
until the objects come back
to another table
some other day.

Position

——— ∞ ———

The gray suits on the street
walk over a black man
asking for cigarette money.
They do not think of him at all
yet offer a gut-reflex of manners
before passing by forever.

Grace

——— ∞ ———

She walks catlike
    on the wrong side of the street.
The air curls up at her touch.
Her deep darkness
    startles onlookers into reverence
the way in which a child
    wavers
        over melted chocolate.
In white, smooth back bared,
    arched beneath the fall colors,
        she keeps pace…
           her face unknown,
           unseen.

Cross Fire

———— ∞ ————

If one is different,
or of a mind to question "Why not?"
is that one not allowed to life
on the same sphere?
What makes it right or just
to club a brother's skull or
rape a sister's soul?
Is the mind of God known
to one select group of worshipers
who determine the destiny
for all who walk their path?
Faith reflects an unseen agreement
'Between God and creation.
Creation turns upon itself
in constant struggle,
in constant need,
in constant greed,
forgetting the bond of humanity,
causing the Creator to mourn
the loss of the temple's sanctity
under a faded lily's light.

Resting by the MLK Display

———— ∞ ————

Enclosed by glass and tempered time
a blackened robe gave comfort.
Not often worn, the fabric
radiated warmth and promise.
The wearer, last enfolded by the robes,
confronted the winds whipping the fabric
forming wings behind him.
He embraced a child or an idea
or his God while in this garment,
as he opposed the bitter
taste of herbs in the wilderness.
Lingering by the case brought peace
from the weary time
as if the wearer stood nearby
in wait of one to take up an unfinished burden.

In Zirconia, North Carolina

————— ∞ —————

The woman stands against the wind
embracing the clouds
and rumbling thunder.
Strands of hair-mist intertwine
whirling the hills into mercy.

Mountain Blessing

———— ∽ ————

The
woodworker
gives a benediction
to a
final piece
he
resurrects
into
what he calls
useful
art.

Wolfe Angel

———— ∞ ————

The stone smile
of an angel
flashes brightly
in Oakdale Cemetery
off Highway 64.
She speaks on the wind's
creative fire.
I sit beneath her bared feet,
waiting for directions
with pen in hand.
She sends me homeward,
ever homeward
where I find my
soul's delight:
a blank page.

Finding a Wolfe

———— ∞ ————

Without knowing the way a river flows,
my feet step lightly through Asheville streets.
I look for Tom, but all I hear
are the modern rhythms of the city.
The Wolfe watches behind the brushing clouds
above the green mountains.
My head tilts in the sunset.
His laughter comes to me in soft ripples
as the darkness falls over Riverside Cemetery.

Connemara Wind Chime

————— ∞ —————

Cattails
stand at attention
near the lake
of the red-white bars and stars
flying above Connemara.
A house on the hill
waits for Sandburg
to come back to a typewriter
on a fruit crate.
Paula's goats roam the farm
without a gentle
dove throat call from the lady of the valley.
The government body cares
for the spirit of the artists
who no longer run
these dimensional fields of grass…
Birds call to those who listen
to the sounds of Connemara.
Boggy frog songs, dragonflies' wings, crickets
sound above the flowing pond.
If Carl and Paula
return for a spell
or a guitar-note
they are not alone.

The land makes us sing a praise to God
for Connemara,
Carl Sandburg's
sweet farm
from long ago.

The Burning of Atlanta

———— ∞ ————

September 17, 1994

A little kerosene burns
early one morning
beneath the canopy of night.
No one has seen the silent one who's torched
Margaret Mitchell's writing
place at 10th and Peachtree.
The burning of Atlanta
takes place while the
town slumbers.
Who is left to mourn the ashes
of a creative spark?
Peggy has the last laugh.
She wanted no monument
to remember her by.
The Dump went the way
of her personal papers:
consumed by orange flame.

Open 24 Hours

————— ∞ —————

Madness
snared in a net
or a caress
in a woman's arms wet
with tears of longing
pulled him along
the foam of the river.
He cannot see where he is going
or which bank will claim him.
Turning in the forces
swirling across his senses
the man demands two eggs
sunny-side up with two charred
strips of bacon
from a tired young waitress
with blond hair.
He asks for nothing more
than sugar in the raw
for fresh coffee
steaming in his eyes.
A stainless steel spoon
stirs the Java jump-start.
The cup meets his lips.
Coffee burns, but he keeps
swallowing, so he will make it to work.

The bills are left under a glass
of untouched water.
The ice is all melted.
He is gone until Monday morning.
She wipes the counter
with a wet rag.

Childhood

Childhood

—————— ∞ ——————

playing with crayons
would be fun
if i could draw my world
without a grown-up
ripping my drawing apart.

Weekend Visitation

———— ∞ ————

On the bay banks I heard my first song,
before industry took away the simple pleasures
of the South Shore.
My father took me to the falls.
We fed Mallards and geese bread from a thirty-nine
cent loaf.
I wanted to stay to hear to see.
He said there wasn't time. It was too cold.
We had to go.
He dropped me in the driveway. I went inside.
He went home.

Overflowing

—————— ∞ ——————

those salty tasting
oozing warmth
ulcer preventing
disgraceful admittance of feeling
humanly divine droplets
known as tears.

Seventeen

————— ∞ —————

Such a creme de la creme
of hope
and
despair.

Tenses

———— ∞ ————

Love
nonexistent
in mortality…
Show me how
to be
needed,
wanted,
loved.

Self-taught

——————— ∞ ———————

a frightened child
running to God
out of blindness
fears
to be open
with Him.

Unspoken

———— ∞ ————

You never said the words, but I heard them
though my ears heard the stillness of cool
indifferent tones.
I heard them sound like a bell's peal
through pine scented thoughts.
Remember moments when you never said the words but
felt them
as you glanced into bedroom eyes,
leaving my love to flow over honeysuckle dreams and
parched realities.
You never said the words,
but neither did I love,
neither did I.

Floridian AM

—————— ∞ ——————

The morning comes.
The morning goes.
Intoxicating as Bacardi rums
Or sand between my toes.

The Inner Flame

——— ∞ ———

I am not more than
a wisp
 of
smoke
to the world,
but
to God
I am a flame of hope and promise
in a darkened room.

Housecleaning

———— ∞ ————

my love
cannot reach me
until I reach
into the inner shadows
of the self.

At Graduation (1984)

———— ∞ ————

Feeling warmly, divinely dillonesque
my mind drifts towards
a conception of a man in
flowing
black robes open to the breeze
welcoming the end of spring.
Taboo to the guilty core,
he invades my moonlit dreams
giving me a world of poets and poses…
leaving me
to put my loss quietly away.

Anne Girl (a dream)

———— ∞ ————

Some nights ago I found myself
in Victorian dress at tea.
The mood I reflected was that of an elf.
A clock showed the time to be three.
Marilla and Matthew and some lovely girl
read "Anne" aloud for our pleasure.
Mother's face mirrored a maddened squirrel.
Her behavior I did not treasure.
I told her to leave…
to stop her whinny shrieking.
She'd rather I'd bereave;
my anger came swiftly peaking.
Anne's words to Racheal Lynde
fell from my lips so loudly.
My "crowd" felt I had not sinned.
My mate never held me so proudly.
La Mere Blanc left her cake on the plate.
We continued our play as before.
Somehow I felt like a brand new slate
my pain erased at the core.

Some Fragrant Jazz

Nina Means "Dear Little One"
(about Nina Cassotto & Bobby Darin)

———— ∞ ————

Dear son:
She never admitted the child as her own,
though she watched, worried,
longing to give the love with which he could soar
higher than both dared to admit.
Dear son:
She nursed her child's fevered body,
but her love extinguished all feeling
as she shared a man with the masses,
making a place for him between sets.
Dear son:
The man turned upon them in bitterness,
running a tired loneliness at the top of the world,
passing her along the way.
Dear son:
The boy called her "sister" until 1 and thirty
years. After her confession
the man dared not say "mother."
Nieces and nephew became sisters and brother
in a gasp for reality before the flame blew out.
The man's father ever faceless
turned the man into the arms of his only child.
Dear son:
the woman wept for the man in the night.

She lost him more than thrice.
His flesh grew cold at death's calling;
his memory grew bright in her eyes.
The masses mourned the star,
but the mother cried silently:
"Dear son."

1993

Sam 1956 and Beyond (SD, Jr.)

———— ∞ ————

Like a sweet warming breeze,
he flew over the decaying rot of racism.
He danced and sang-smiles all smiles...
fooling all into thinking he was some
lowerthandirtuppity...
He fought to heal sickness,
distracting you with melodies.
Sometimes he hated you back,
not letting on;
sometimes he loved you and
(surprise!)
you loved him back.
Down came the racial barrier:
costs blood and sweat.
Show's over.
Barrier's up just in time for a day to day reality.
He could not go where you could.
You kicked him some more.
Black and blue,
bleeding life
he made it over the wall.
He joyfully danced in the sun as you whispered,
"Why is he trying to be white?"
Never seeing him, you threw him in a pile with Cole,
taking for granted the simple freedoms he fought for

and the joys he brought.
`Neath the soul's frail cover existed human worth.
Let him be now.
Let him rest.
Retract the teeth and claws.
You can't hurt him any more.

Lady Night

———— ∞ ————

Billie Holiday reached for a star
and brought it down to earth.
In our collective psyche
her mellow instrument
reprised memories
of ballads azure.

Honey-Cole

His coffee hands poured over keys
forming flowered rhapsodies.
Warmly whispered fragrant jazz
exposed a coolness no one has.
Timely elegance altered fashion,
offering blossoms tinged with passion.
Sweet jasmine chords impressed on wax,
opened a hive then closed to blacks.
A gentle soul in a land of white
said Madison Avenue was afraid of the night.
A garden of children wove a pride
his outstretched arms held close beside.
Early winter chilled the riff
which paused to ponder an untimely if.

Jazz Men in Hotlanta

———— ∞ ————

A young man's voice
floats along night currents
as youthful as juniper in flower,
as knowing as the dust on an aging bottle
of bourbon in New Orleans.
His band of angels gather to play heaven and earth
on a handful of instruments
of metal and wood before the dawning of southern
      kisses in summer.

Sinatra Sonata

———— ∞ ————

The woodwinds blow full force,
though not as youthful or polished as in yesterdays.
The knowledge grows thorny roses
for the public to snatch from a private garden.
His steps rush madly through a wall of people.
Ever onward he wanders
like a Roman vine in harvest,
pouring wine in many cups
at many tables
before the last call
silences the man
who leaves
a voice
to comfort weeping strangers.

The Offering

A woman gives a handful of roses
to a hero she thought she'd never see.
He returns a lavender silk to her soiled, thorn-
pricked hands.
A woman takes it from the aging chairman
to keep it to wipe her brow,
when she feels less than loved.

Reflective Nature

Autumn

———— ❧ ————

In a leafy,
misty waltz,
I'm a nymph
on the run.
Onlookers bristle
at such exuberance,
yet I laugh
as if I
were a brook
passing over
jagged rocks.
I am in the
color of life,
knowing, too,
I will die
with the leaves.
I will not fear
the morrow.
Rather, I will taste
the wine of the moment
for that is all I have.

The Wood

———— ∞ ————

Against the grain of elder wood,
the frenzied growth of youthful weeds,
I stand my earth in quiet protest
reaching heaven with branches outstretched.

C-A-T

little
tiger
cat
grab my heart like a catnip mouse.
play and chew until my will is your plaything to
torment.
little
tiger
cat
stalk my soul like a leaf on the lawn.
pounce and capture until my mind is your mouse-
     trap to command.

The Garden

———— ∞ ————

Bamboo.
Graceful,
foreign,
kingly
crowns
the yard of a Southern daughter's home,
stripping majesty
from the English Ivy.

Southbound Snowfall

———— ∞ ————

Snow
falls from the sky
to cover the ground
with a fine lace blanket.

Winter Morning

—————— ∞ ——————

In the quiet dawn
on the mountain
God smiles once more.
The sun peers from the east
as a great, curious child would
who is caught by
the wonder of discovery.
Soft, white powder
covers the landscape
where deer fed
in the mysterious night before
when lovers
snuggled deep
within their quilts.

On the Trail

———— ∞ ————

Embers
of starlight
smolder
by the camp
beneath a night canopy.
The soles of my boots burn.
I keep them on the edge
between warmth and death.
A wolf calls. Then another.
I cry back,
answering the bridge
between here and there.

New World Order

———— ∞ ————

When we cease making useless belongings
which clutter the earth
we will find our way home again.

Death of a Georgia Farm, June 1993

———— ∞ ————

A child's kite flies overhead...
the ripped, red Georgia slope.
A blue kite by the Scenic Highway descends
twisted, churned, and choked.
And still the men build a faster route
between one town and another.
"We need jobs. It's either the land or the people,"
they say.
If the land is taken,
what becomes of the creatures?
How far must they keep moving?
Further out the beasts withdraw
as the men push onward.
No peace. No real purpose
but to keep moving the flow of people
and money.

Death of a Georgia Farm, Part Two, October 1994

A race began
on a gray ribbon
set in place
across the death knoll
of a farm
admired from the driver's side.
Quiet stirrings
keep people racing from Snellville
to the Bethesda chimney
baseball diamond
where children play
in the open spaces
of grass and iron dust
sticking to their
bright uniforms.
The absent lives
leave a hole within a girl
as she searches the
empty horizon for a wild creature
thrown from the sight of men chasing themselves
around a diamond,
keeping careful score
over a tangible figure
amounting to little
for the ones doing all the running.

Crane On the Rock

————— ∞ —————

The waterfowl stands on a rock
as the river surges past with the roar of a
misplaced ocean
calling,
ever calling me away from the urban life.
The bird stands alone and it is natural for him to
       sun himself on a golden afternoon.
Free from an Autumn chill,
he moves all around…
changing perspective…
on one foot or the other.
He holds on as I return.
I have less determination
than he.

Christmas Prison

———— ∽ ————

The government
shutdown
stole the park
away from me
as if I were
Native-born.
No more will
I be permitted
to hike or
walk the riverbank trails.
My heart breaks
with disbelief as my
child's faith
evaporates
beside a locked gate.
Who can own a river?
Men…
without vision
carve and plan and plot.
All I want to do is walk
with God.
It seems I have to go
within to find him.
They've barred me
from holy ground…
leaving me to wander
in paved lots.

Chattahoochee River Walk

———— ∞ ————

Into the woods I wander.
No compass. No map for a guide.
The sun hidden through a thicket of trees.
A cemetery of Southern dust.
No kin to me, I pay my respects and move on,
becoming more lost on public land
that once was private.
What native stood on this land before
the Southerner?
I wonder who will stand in my place before long.

American Holocaust

The words are not mine
but I know them in my mind.
Water, air, mother earth, eagle,
sky, sun, moon, animal spirits
lead me away from this
stone jungle.
Failing to blend, I fight
to walk beside the river.
Baptism is not far from me.
A student forever
I take the herb from the wild and the
		peace from the sky.
Slow walks through
wind songs smooth the roughness
of a false life…
collecting, not giving,
running, not searching.
A pebble in the shoe
is a big stone
breaking the stride
in a stooped walk.
Broken words are a prison.
Come together
before we are an echo.

Intuition

In Search of Self

———— ∞ ————

Going along the lonely way,
I become more night than day.
With face tilted toward a pensive moon,
the path to home is forged that soon.

Change

———— ∞ ————

alone,
without a crumb or crust to eat
I shiver
and wait
for my spirit to open
in flight
so I may escape
without a trace of my existence.

Human Frailty

————— ∞ —————

The quiet mask
drops off my face.
Before I can recover
gracefully
the mask
shatters into one thousand
pieces on the floor
b
  e
    l
      o
        w
the constant ugly murmurs
of gossips.

Fools

———— ∞ ————

Fools never try
to find answers
to difficult questions
or ponder the universe
or thank God
or admire a rainbow
or live each moment
as it comes.

Treasure Hunt

———— ∞ ————

To seek
every day
miracles
in the most mundane tasks
holds the magic of
all possibility.

Evolution

———— ∞ ————

What will happen?
Why worry.
Just don't sit there
in a complacent daze.
Do something positive!
Disassemble the negative illusion
using the power
within your
human shell.
Be aware…
if you dare.

Uncertainty

———— ∞ ————

Uncertainty
means you have
stepped off the cliff...
into the great divide
between
what is predictable
and what is not.

Illusion

———— ∞ ————

We are not
who we
appear
to be
on the
surface
of life.
We are
oneness
in the
cradle of
the
universe.

The Strength to Go On

———— ∞ ————

The strength to go on
can be found
inside a lonely selfhood…
dormant,
unchecked,
sleeping.

An Artist's Prayer

O Creator, great light and
giver of inspiration,
help us to find our way
back to you.
Help us to focus on the
creative spirit.
Keep us from losing ourselves
in the dark, cold ego.
Keep us on the path
of well being.
Help us to be aware.
Embrace us and teach us to
love others as well as ourselves.
Teach us surrender.
Pick us up when we fall.
Help us find beauty
and contentment in creativity.
Allow us to nurture others.
Guide us through life.
We are all connected.
We are all from You.
We hold You above all.
Come into our hearts
as we serve others joyfully.
Amen.

Angels

———— ∞ ————

Angels catch
the quiet remark
when the speaker
feels alone.
Following each movement
they press fiery
wings
around the human
frailty.

Kodak Moments

In Brian's Light

———— ∞ ————

written as a memory for Brian's mother
26th June 1991

In the mirror of the world,
I see the vibrant light of a spirit
warming friends
in a wild orange blaze
of laughter and lucent youth,
against the cold-hearted darkness
of conformity.

Aida's Door

Somewhere
A door waits to be found
by a person in search of another person
unseen by the eyes,
but known to the heart.
Moments stolen
pass too quickly
and the seeker wonders if the door exists
or if it is a foolish myth.
Sometime
the warmth invades the bitter taste
of being left to search
alone.
Some way
the pursuer will find the key
to the love she sought
courageously.

Dad

———— ∞ ————

A quality passed from you keeps me alive.
In the end that quality won out
as I am here to tell the tale.
You are a survivor,
a cowboy,
a sailor if you will.
Someone I can never emulate.

Michelle

———— ∞ ————

You are all the wonderful,
magical, translucent
powers of God
in one lovely,
fresh-faced woman
who stands
on the front lines
of a classroom
in Columbia, SC
day after day
turning on the
lights behind
forty pairs of shining
eyes.

Nora

My sister,
the artist's flame
burns within
thy mortal chamber
to help fellow wanderers
find their way home.

Little Red Keds

———— ∞ ————

(for Kenny Rozwat)

little red keds
once kicked a ball.
little red keds
were bright and small.
little red keds are empty tonight.
The boy who wore them
ran out of sight.

Miles, age 2

———— ∞ ————

My arms open
in a floodgate of love
mingled with open laughter…
for Mi
touches my pain
and down it falls.

My Cousin Missy

———— ∞ ————

She danced through the valley of youth
a blossom to be savored
not pressed in a book
with dead petals falling to the floor.

Meridith Nights

———— ∞ ————

The honky-tonk angel sings to a roping lover.
She lassos his heart
with golden fire
wrapped around blue denim.
The frost comes through the barn door
catching the bed of hay
warmed by lovers
dimming dusty skies.

Heather

———— ∞ ————

a vision

When your graceful,
golden strength moved
my love to surface
you were at once
sister, daughter,
wunderkind supreme.
If you never
see my face,
hear my voice
or know my life…
it matters not.
God brought you
on the
breath of a vision, Heather.
And it was enough.

Homeless Cat

———— ∞ ————

in a box
he lives.
he mews at me.
sometimes I rush by.
sometimes I feed him.
he always greets me.
I don't always see him
when he's here.
a tail twitches,
a purr sounds,
but I've already gone for the day.

Dorothy: 1946

———— ∞ ————

Under the light
of a half-caste
lantern
the woman   '
arranges
her hat
with her left
hand
while her right
hand fumbles
for a cigarette
in a frayed,
burgundy purse.
She's just
left apartment four-B
where her man
lies asleep
beneath a blanket.
Dorothy shivers
before stepping
across a crack
in the pavement.

Home Away

———— ∞ ————

In the kitchen with Silvi
I feel at home.
The cabinets shine
with warm, bright wood…
Warm to the touch as
the uncut loaf on the white countertop.
Bread to eat,
to warm myself over
while I listen
to this incredible woman
spin the oral history
of the world.
She shows me who I
could be if given
a chance to grow
in her sun.

He and She

———— ∞ ————

(for K. & S.)

In the bright light of the sun
two people love one another,
taking pleasure from
willing lips and eyes
which know the depth
of a rare joining
many never experience.
Anyone can see the
beauty between
the woman and the man
for their spirits bloom,
rising to glory
before nightfall
closes the petals
until morning.

Inez: a preface to motherhood

———— ∞ ————

She sits and writes inside
four walls
away from her students'
questioning, arched eyebrows.
Her newest student
turns downward
in the fluid kingdom
as if to endlessly
challenge
Inez's fine mind
and high sense of humor.
Inez knows she is up
for the journey.
Now is the time
for reflection
before divine deliverance.
Inez meets each morning
in a state of grace.
When? When? How long?
"Near spring," she answers
quietly.
All she can do is wait
for her baby's eyes
to meet her own.
In that instant
she will fall in love
all over again.

Ruth

———— ∞ ————

She carries
a camera
to common places.
Ruth freezes
a moment
for all time
in icy black and white
images on Kodak paper.
She is a strong,
smiling woman
with a mission
to develop life
as she finds it.

The Magi

———— ∞ ————

He lights his cigarette
the way Astaire
walked across a lonely sound stage.
He speaks with the tongue of an angel.
People gather around him
as if he holds the secret of life
in his back pocket.
Aldo knows all
but says nothing
unless you are brave enough
to meet his wry gaze.
Just remember this.
Get out of the way before
the truth runs over you.

The Free Man

———— ∞ ————

The truly free man
forever bound
to the land
takes nothing
but photographic images
and a seasonal bounty
from the harvest.
He gives back
compost scraps,
broken wood,
bits of seeds.
He believes
in leaving
nothing behind
but
creative memory.

Serina

———— ∞ ————

Dark hair frames
butterfly magic
in her eyes
as they stare
past an open window.
The rain splashes
through, but
Serina doesn't move…
doesn't blink.
Her mind forever
pushes forward…
Exploring
every possibility
available to
a goddess
in repose.

Thomas Wolfe

———— ∞ ————

He
walked
alone in a downpour
of thoughts
and
wrote
millions of words
for scholars to sift
and
he
laughed
from the depths
of a
writer's emptiness.

Belinda and the Editor

———————— ∞ ————————

Oh, my God.
Where did you come from?
Oh, it doesn't matter.
I've got your letters
in a box and
dear lady,
I promise to read every one of them
and edit each with care.
What's this?
You left a memoir behind?
Oh, God.
Oh, my God.
This is too much.
You really are too incredible
to be collecting dust.
Come into the light again.
Tell me your story
and I will listen carefully
and take notes like a madman.
What's that you say?
Go girl.
You go.

Dori (dor e)

———— ∞ ————

n. 1. farmer fever. 2. storyteller spinning. 3. mind meditative. 4. cook combining. 5. sassy sister. 6. Informal. A remarkable woman. Honey, honey, there are more peaches to be gathered.

Nocturne

————— ∞ —————

Fifteen pounds
of black cat
sleeps on
my chest.
A contented
kitty smile
curls his
whiskers.
His pink
tongue peeks out
from hiding.
He looks so
stuffed and harmless
until one
cat's eye
opens
eternal mystery.

Home Again

In Purling, New York
a house of dreams
stands
boarded up
by neglect.
Once lovers met
in secret and
children climbed
sapling branches.
Now homeless men camp
beneath the rising pillars
and tell stories
around a threshold fire.

Inside a Woman's Head

Sister CFS

She
stood
in
the
same
check out
line
as
me.
She
said
she
had
painful
symptoms
and
sometimes
felt
like
all
life
was
gone.
"Do
you

have
CFS?"
I
asked.
"Yes,"
she
said.
"So
do
I."
We
understood
one
another
without
exchanging
names
or
phone
numbers
because
we'd
been
to
the
same
drop-off
point.

Haus Frau

In the garden
I grow crazy.
Legs spindly
and wild heart lazy.
The mind will harden
and then get hazy.
What's a gal to do?

Summer Love Revisited

———— ∞ ————

A child
fell
into
love
one
evening.
She
followed
a man
home.
A woman
woke
up
one
morning.
She
packed
a suitcase
and left
with
no regrets.

Siren's Lullaby

———— ∞ ————

A smile is a deceptive life mask
or an outright expression
of happiness pursued
or seduction clouded
in memory.
Witch grass bow to the king's wind.
Bounce back and slap his face.
Throw back your head,
Thrust both breasts out,
Sing the song
to drive him mad.
Tart, sweet, sexual temptress
on the rocky shelf
abandon the safety net
where fish are caught and sold.
Swim freely through
shark infested waters
until the sweet island
can be stood upon
with love's bare children
washed by cold, salty wombs
and rocked to seaweed lullabies.

Helpmate

———— ∽ ————

Is there a man out there
who could love a woman
with ovarian cancer?
Would his hands move
fluidly down her
shapely, seductive
belly to the
"portal of the soul?"
Would he look into
her eyes
as he did
during the silent spring
of their love making
or would he turn away
from her body's revolt?
Is there a man out there
who could love a woman
whose breasts have been
surgically removed?
Would his hands caress
the scarred bony chest
of the woman standing beside him?
Let the answer be yes.

Give Mama A Little Sugar

He raised his fist to
his wife in the
howling darkness
and she cried
because she did not
block his punches
fast enough in the third round.
She cursed him
as her body
doubled-over
in the shape
of a slender,
silver nutcracker.

All Out At Whistle Stop

I want to be where Idgie Threadgoode is
and run and play in the wild wood,
picking honey out
of a great oak tree.
I want to eat a plate
of Fried Green Tomatoes
swimming in milk gravy
and talk to Miss Ruth
about the afterlife.
Sipsey's voice will rise from
the kitchen like light
biscuits waiting for the sunny
butter to roll down the sides onto a blue plate
and Big George will make
the best barbecue in Alabama.
Smoky Lonesome will share a plate
with me in the exit light of evening.
We spin tales of Railroad Bill as Idgie slips
past us with coal dust on
her face like a panther
on the run.

Down in the Mouth

———— ∞ ————

strange to be
a prisoner of the body:
missing tasks,
feeling undone
by a silent battle waiting
to be won.

Just a Thought

————— ∞ —————

Tiger teeth
and eyes that shine,
a mother's guilt they say is mine.
A long ivy wreath
ties me,
binds me
just like twine.
Now I wish the pain would wilt,
so I would run clear and free,
behaving more like little me.

Transformation

———— ∞ ————

The moon cried out in pain
against the splintered plain.
The child named Insane
will not come home again.
To wander in the rain,
to wash the old blood stain,
the child came from Cain
on the wings' hopeless wane.

Mistress to Mistress

———— ∞ ————

The first woman
watched
him closely.
He said
nothing
from the
marsh.
His eyes
burned
brown,
uncertain
of the
outcome
by a
summer
pond.
The bloom
in her
had been
stolen by
some merciless
illness,
yet
the first woman
spoke with

great favor.
"You may
have him.
I don't
want him
to suffer,
but you cannot
have my home
or my name."
Admiring
her honesty
the other woman calmly
answered,
"I do not
want what
is rightfully
yours.
My only desire
is to
love him."
He stirred
in the moment
as the other woman
looked into
the first woman's
courageous eyes.
Satisfied
with his choice,
the first woman
sent them away.

Written on the Heart

—————— ∞ ——————

(for Lyn)

A letter came
and I sensed
the contents
beneath folded white pages
were not social notes
for another keeper of the house
The contents spilled
on the paper's face.
Blood on the body
mended the spirit
as you ran
with a poet
across the
porous snow.

Song of the Unpublished

——— ∞ ———

At the base of despair
I find myself with two
cups in hand.
One is empty, dry as dust...
the other chipped,
still holding
the nectar of life which
I've lost my taste for.
My belly ties itself in knots
before the fear slams me on the head.
Shame covers me.
The blank page cackles.
A pen runs dry.
My life is over
until I try.

Angel in the Wind

———— ∞ ————

Angel in the wind stay steady,
Until my heart cries, "I'm ready."
We'll fly to forever
on a wild endeavor…
a trip which makes mortals quite heady.

Jupiter Summer

———— ∞ ————

Orbit my free breathing waist
and leave a trail of
cosmic desire before
Jupiter explodes into
a sun or
some such miracle.

Oktoberfest

———— ∞ ————

The window of his soul
catches me and
once again I fall
into swirling October leaves
to meet the warm, dark earth
of Catawba.
In his quiet way
he tosses my stone-heart
into the silent undercurrents
between us.
I look into his
luminous eyes
for answers
only to find more questions.

Note from a Surviving Twin

———— ∞ ————

Mother,
do not be
afraid
to love me
while I'm
with you.
I know
you still
grieve
for my
brother,
but let
me become
a woman
instead of
remaining
the little
girl you
were afraid
would die.
I won't
break,
Mother.
Honest.
Love,
J.

Paper Affair

A Letter

---∞---

a letter…a letter
what could be better?
to have and to hold…
to read and refold…
to keep in a box…
open or under locks.

Confession to a Faceless Man

———— ∞ ————

I love you in darkness
and wake with you each morning.
Long walks into the night
fail to shake your spirit from mine.
To say I love you with passion's kisses…
To taste the sweetness of you…
To make love with you soulfully
ignites a dormant winter's frost in my breast.
Sit with me in the firelight, my beloved.
Warm yourself within me.
I love no other.

Soul Mates

———— ∞ ————

Wire-gold rims
hide two fire-lit eyes
taking me down a road
of divine emotion.
You know me first in sunlight.
Without a word
you make me silent.
Our lips will merge
before we ever touch.
I know we've each
come home when we speak.
Love me into darkness
and let me be your
starry-eyed muse.
Create life and art
within the garden of passion.
Begin the season's recognition
when next you look into
my soul.

Meteor Showers

—————— ∞ ——————

A handful of stars
fell from the sky
one Texas night.
Your blazing fire
soared before the horizon
as I whispered,
"Beloved."
The pavement sparked
today's meeting as
Carolina dawn
found eyes
fluttering awake
on a cold morning.
I wished on as many showers
as I could count.
Slumber overtook me as
you entered
a realm
without boundary
or space.

White Wolf

—————— ∞ ——————

A wolf with
flashing eyes
saw the hearts
of men and women
who ceased being.
He grieved for their
joyousness as he
followed the scent
of mystery.
Blood racing
through him
came from
his mother's
secret womb.
The fever drew
him back until
her wild beauty
touched her son's
restless nature.
Primal memory
jarred
the white wolf
and he stood
quietly contemplating
some trouble
he could get into.

Recognition

——————— ∞ ———————

Without warning
you come to me
in the night.
I feel your breath
on my neck.
You say nothing
before your lips find mine.
We fall into one another;
we become a new being
and though we are
complete
within ourselves
a sweetness blooms
between us
because we have found one
another's restful,
timeless pulse.

The Art of Fine Craftsmanship

——— ∞ ———

His God-given
weathered hands
shaped me into
another object
of desire.
No longer woman
I became a sail
being raised
to kiss the wind.
Then I was transformed
into a warm
piece of sweet maple wood.
Beneath his touch
I became
a creative
earth mother
formed by wood, fire,
pollen, water, honey,
snow, and autumn leaves.
He walked through
my woods,
marveling at everything
around him.
In that instant
I worked him
and he changed
beneath my touch.

Reconcilable Differences

He wears the earth's colors
while I wear the sky's.
He comes from Southern clay
while I was born to Northern shores.
He travels the road
while I wait by the fire.
He is the poet's soul
while I am the poet.
He chops wood
while I write on paper.
He carries the strength of the Blue Ridge
while I am the smoke rising above him.
He burns red-hot
while I simmer slowly.
He takes me into his arms
while I forget the world.

Insight

———— ∞ ————

He knew
they had
been one
before
he saw
her coming
to the
mountain
He waited
for her
by a
pile of
dusty
books.
When
she wasn't
looking
he tucked
her
business card
close
to
his body
and

she knows now
it was
then
when he
first
undressed
her soul.

Taster's Choice

———— ∞ ————

You are
full flavored
coffee
to be
sipped
by a
green,
vibrant
tea
drinker.

Cabin Fever

———— ∞ ————

In a cabin
the wilderness
entered their bodies
where an enchantment
followed them into the bedroom.
The lovers
bayed at a full,
crisp moon
set so snugly
in a black sky
wet with ancient desires.

En Route

———— ∞ ————

The desire to float
came over me
on the aisle
of a Delta 727.
I would become
liquid passion
rolling towards you,
raining on your smooth body
until we came together
during a forest storm.
I shall stoke your fire.
You will stir my embers.
What combustion
awaits
two glorious
dreamers
who know
no better.

Two Candles

———— ∞ ————

Candles burn slowly
when lit by a match.
Wax drips on
tender fingers
kissed by a poet's soul.
In a flash
a formless
hot pool
spills across
a wooden top
and quickly hardens.

Before the Snows Came

———— ∞ ————

When you left me so
wrapped up in white cotton
wanting more,
I could only bear
to watch you walk away
from me.
If I had seen you drive away
my feet would have run
across the cold, tar pavement.
Then I would have become
your goddess in bed linen.
At every stop along the highway
we'd make crazy love,
unearth every current,
and shock the meek
onlookers
driving slowly past
the perfect spectacle.

Notation

———— ❧ ————

Too moved to write
another line of poetry
all I can do is
blow you a kiss on the wind.
May you feel my warm lips
come upon you swiftly
so all words cease
before passions take over.

Within His Heart

————— ∞ —————

He keeps a woman
within his heart.
No one sees her.
No one knows her face
but the man
she loves from so far away.
He kissed her once
in passing.
She tasted good to him then.
Together they were
wintergreen
in January.
He keeps watch
on the height of the thermostat.
He burns for the woman
in secret and
cannot be open
with their passion.
He is wise to keep
the woman
to himself.
No one may take her
from him.
Not even death.

Letter Head

———— ∞ ————

A beautiful book
of letters arrived last night.
They were written and drawn for other women.
I wanted your words.
Why did you hide behind a book
when your wilderness songs
were the sounds I craved?

Upon Waking

———— ∞ ————

You come to me
in dreams of wild flight.
Your strong arms
carry me into oblivion.
Wish we could stay there
for a time
sitting on a cloud
conjured up
by fantastic schemes.
Upon waking
your scent lingers
and I cry a little
over sheets wet with longing.

At the Core of Humanity

————— ∞ —————

You
are
basically
Earth,
Air,
Water,
Nature,
Faith,
Mind,
Heart,
Soul,
Compassion,
Being.

The River Dance

———— ∽ ————

I am
your bridge
to a
place you've
never been.
You are
the uncharted
river flowing
to the
Gulf Stream.
Take me
down the
dark waters.
I come
with you
so willingly.
Let us
travel to
the mouth
where white
hot sand
meets torrid
blue currents.

Epitaph

Three Fates

—————— ∞ ——————

A spool of thread
unwound in the dark
spans the breadth
of the room.
Hands pull at the thread,
plucking the woven
live wire as a musician
plays with the strings of a lute.
A pair of shears
cuts the thread
stilling the song of life
as it falls to the floor.

Epitaph

In the urban asphalt jungle
do I sit and wait for you.
Under a gray marble slab
I try to pen a thought or two.
If the thought blows away
or is struck by snow,
remember I was here
to tell you it was so.

Individuality

———— ∞ ————

Do you see yourself
as less than you are?
How unique
and apart
you are
from the
rest
of the crowd.
Rejoice
in all
you are
for you can be no less
than true
to yourself.

The Burning of Atlanta

————— ∞ —————

12 May 1996

They came after
Peggy's writing place
like a thief
with a torch
and a lingering
stench of kerosene.
The cinders
have clung
after the rain
of firemen
without
the evidence
of courage
on the part
of the
torchbearer.

Epitaph

Statistic

———— ∞ ————

The terror
comes
ripping my
screaming
head
apart.
There's
not a trace
of myself
for you to find.
Soon
memory dims
and no one can say
if my hair
was red or blonde
or if I may have been
rich or poor,
black or white.
You have
my story
on video tape
to replay
for amusements
sake.

Coming Out

———— ∞ ————

My chrysalis:
lustrous, green…
wrapped tightly
around me.
I am cloaked
in darkness
still yet
asleep
while other
butterflies
dry
their big,
colorful
wings.

Gettysburg

————— ∞ —————

We have battles
to win
and men to bury.
Do not give us
pretty words.
We have no use
for them here.
Take your glory,
gentlemen.
The hell with glory,
gentlemen.
To hell with you.
You began this bloodletting.
We labor to finish
the war.

In the B & B

————— ∞ —————

I am a kept woman
on the backstairs.
I am a formless,
v
   a
      porous,
bare back phoenix
reclined
in wait
for the dark man
to return
from the mornings hunt.

Maryanne: 1769

———— ∞ ————

Into the sea
she was tossed
far away from thee.
Her fair countenance lost
to painters, poets, and he.
Down she goes at a terrible cost
to both you men, but she's free!

The Unmade Bed

In this room I slept
freely and unafraid.
In my heart silent
dreams I kept
while future plans
were being made.

Wolfe Pack

———— ∞ ————

Julia?
Mabel?
Fred?
Ben?
Oh, Ben is that you?
Are you visions
or ghostly memories
from some other time?
You gather in a circle,
huddled in the afternoon
meadow of death.
The coffin has not come.
The grass is still green
beneath our feet.
Have you waited all
day in your Sunday clothes
for the tardy one
to return?
No one will
be buried
this September day.
W.O. is long gone,
strolling with Cynthia along the shore.
Look for Tom lounging behind chiseled
      monuments or whispering over

a writer's shoulder.
He's roaming the earth
and writing all the words
he hadn't thought of before.
Oh, yes, he'll come home.
But not today, Miss Julia.
Not today.

The Sculptor

———— ∞ ————

Until
you found
your woman
behind closed doors
your arms held the wind,
the changeling,
the aura
of the unknown
human factor.
You looked into her eyes
for reassurance and found
the sweeping vortex
of mutual attraction.
Are you aware of
your part in shaping
the still wet clay?
Your knowing hands
have touched the face
of uncertainty.

The Upper Room

So much of you
runs clear
this morning.
You hold me
so close
and I can't feel
any emotion
beneath a blanket
of shock.
It is natural
to be here,
so surreal, and yet
I keep my focus
on faces covering
the walls
and on the door
to nowhere.
You are here and I hold fast
to life
as I pray for
death to pass.
We fracture and
bleed a little
as you plow deeper
into the earth,

Epitaph

turning the soil
to the sky.
Warmed, I pull you
closer,
no longer
fearing the outcome.

The Gambrell Women

———— ∞ ————

Without a sound
the women
rise in the
early morning
as they have always done.
Breakfast and soft
conversation
journey over
the table.
A mother
and first-born…
the quiet one…
share fragments
of themselves.
Then
the daughter
charges through
darkness
rolling into
light
on her way to work.
Across town third-born…
the strong one…
settles into
the rhythms of

the same morning.
She'll call
to hear
just how
her mother's day is
coming along
as their laughter
tumbles
across
the phone wires.
Fewer dishes
fill the sink.
A mother remembers
her faraway son with fire blue eyes
and a husband
who lingers
between the now and the veil.
The women
are one
throughout
the days.
When they
return home,
they enter a
country house
run with conviction
and painted
with vivacity.

The Great Mystery

———— ∞ ————

I have read
dying is like
going to sleep
and waking up
without a body.
We're all there…
Complete.
Observing.
Divine.
Bathed in the glory
of unconditional love.
Why must we wait
until dying
to rise?
We are connected
and never alone
as long as we
open to the
one power
within each and all.

Following Angels and Wolves

Letting Go

Time to be angry,
then sad,
and quiet.
A little girl
with scraped knees
on the street.
One valise
stands upright
clothes locked up tight.
No where to go.
No way to know.

The Donation

———— ∞ ————

In the Salvation Army center
are the photographs
you gave me.
I framed both, then
I showed both
to people who passed through
my life
as if you were with me always.
When I caught you with another
I burned your letters
and removed my pictures
from my walls.
If it is simple to erase them,
why is it difficult to get over
your phantom love?

Synchronicity

———— ∞ ————

No matter where I go,
you are there
in other faces, in other traces
of passing men.
The three act comedy we live
separately closes down.
I push you outside myself.
You appear
over and over
until I die of laughter.

Divine Healing

———— ∞ ————

Before waking
the thunderous
flutter of Angels
brush against
a broken body
caught in
a deep rip-tide
of a spouse's neglect.

Standing Up

───────── ∽ ─────────

We come to one another
as if we've been
in the same embrace all along.
You teach
a wayward girl
to embrace
her complete self.
The lesson
will be
a long time
coming.
Your pupil
tends to be
thick-minded
and
battle worn.
You love
to
teach
but before
it is all
over,
know
you
are

the
one
who
will
be
the
student.

On the Trail in Round Top, NY

———— ∞ ————

Lost in a rocky meadow
surrounded by a stillness
not heard before,
I know I will find
my heart's desire
deep within
the moment
at hand.

Madison Rivers

———— ∞ ————

In a rainstorm
he showed
a wisdom beyond his twenties.
The black knight
cut through ancient Southern mores.
He stood among them
at a lunch counter
and said,
"Ignore them.
They won't
bother us
if you
don't make
it an "issue."
We sat side by side
and ordered
coffee with cream.
Madison comes in memory.
I can't believe
he's dust today,
back in the earth
so soon after being born.
To die from AIDS
so prematurely

no voice in the house?
no smile backstage?
Our friend is gone.
No more. No more.

Winter Coat at 48 Spruce Street

———— ∞ ————

Dear Man,
how I would love
to wrap myself
inside your magic coat
and feel the warmth
of your pockets
as I bury myself
every inch deeper
until winter's night
passes on.
Woman

The Rogue Hunter

In the doorway
I saw you
as the hunter
you've always been.
Find a woman.
Take aim.
Roll her in the glade
until she cries your name.
Then return her spent body
to the woods of longing
before you slink back
into the brush
as you wait for
the next gazelle.

Sunday

————— ∞ —————

A special magic
overcomes the stress
from the week before
when you remember
everything which occurred
has passed away
and once again you can start
the day
with no mistakes
in the way.

Ruth II

————— ∞ —————

She is a much stronger lady
than I saw before.
one with grit,
humor,
and grace.
Ruth is capable
of loving the shadow
as she is of loving
the light.
She takes pictures of the soul
as well as the body.
Don't be surprised if you are displayed upon
her wall one day.
F-L-A-S-H!

Coffee Break

My arms
hold you
although you rush
around
never stopping long enough
to secure
a conversation
or a throaty kiss
from dreamy lips
you once found
melon-ripe
at mid-night.
Contemplate over coffee.
Recall how our steam rose,
our sugar spilled,
and our creamed flowed.
Have you ever missed
the jolt I'd give
you throughout the day
or are you just happy to just
go cold turkey?
Are we a connection
or sexually addicted,
misplaced persons?

I ask,
but you have a silent answer
which stuns the
heart
until it shrivels
up.

Tina Dunne Gambrell

———— ∞ ————

Unaffected
by
the
outside
she
is
basic
like
dark
bread
or
a
spring
garden
or
smiling
babies.
She
loves
without
question.
Her
grown
children
bless

The
last
person
she
thinks
of
is
her.
How
blissfully
unaware
Tina
is
of
her
invaluable
worth.

her
but
Tina
wants
more
children
to
fill
her
lap.
It
is
her
dream
to
see
everyone
happy.

Fred Chappell

(sorry Fred, I'm a confessional poet)

Behind
a mountain
of books
he sneaks
a peek
at the
folks who
are his readers.
The smile
in his
voice
turns
up
the volume
and we
forget to
get books
signed
because—
damn it all—
Fred puts
us under
a spell.

Blowing Rock Snow

———— ∞ ————

The black birds
are my companions
I am their keeper
of seed and feed
during November
silver moments
shivering into
yesterday's
nighthawk
Go away
leave me
to the birds
we understand
what this time
of hermitage
means
Down
Down
Down
white powder
lull me
in the
mountain cry
I remember
so well.

Twin Birth

———— ∞ ————

for my brother

We are told
we are born alone
but I do not believe this.
My brother
broke the birth canal.
A blue ring circled
his head?
a halo,
a birthing wound,
a karmic mark.
The doctors
let it go as
as they found
a hidden placenta
way in the back.
They couldn't
stir a breath in me.
My heart
would not respond.
Someone made a choice
and I came alive.
We were placed
in cases filled with

oxygen and warmth.
My blond twin ate food
as I was fed
with an eyedropper.
Father McPhail
administered
baptism on two souls
behind glass.
My parents
suffered the
way parents suffer
when there is talk
of small white caskets.
Warren P. died
the next day and
was buried in the Coast Guard cemetery.
Never was he mentioned
to me, his sister
but I knew,
I knew a missing part
of Joan M.
emancipate.

Saturday Night At The Cosmic Coffee House

Cinnamon roll
goes round and round.
A musical son
dances around his father
who waits at the table.
On men's night out
they meet over sweet mocha dreams.
Mama's home in the quiet night air.
She is breathing for a change.
The two men get louder
when they slice into the sugar-wet roll.
They are the same being,
both children at once.

Jennifer and Friend

———— ∞ ————

Who knows what's at the bottom
of a clear person?
She's been hurt like you.
Somehow you met on the main street of Boone
and struck up a conversation
which never really ends.
You go back and forth about life and men
and what's at the beginning of the universe.
We are women, that's all…
but that's everything.
She is a mirror
but looks nothing like you.
Jennifer's free-spirited laughter
let loose in the mountains.
You go out with her
and have a beer, which you only do
with your father.
She accepts you with your faults and
you accept her friendship unconditionally.
For the first time in a long time
you don't have to explain yourself.
Main Street grows darker,
the glasses empty.
All the talk stills
and you are both happy

to go your own ways,
free to meet at some
unspecified time
when talk will resume
where it left off.

The Vacant Heart

———— ∽ ————

You had been there
for me a long time ago.
These days I face
a mountain.
Sometimes my flaccid body
releases a sigh.
I curse myself
for loving someone who
cares less and less
in the barren frost
of love turned bitter.
Inattention is a mallet
striking me down once more.
I attract men who see me as a
pretty weed free from care,
altogether hearty,
ready for
mowing down
or picking up.
I shall tend
my own garden
and keep
Lady Chatterley's lover
out.

Camille Claudine

———— ∞ ————

Throwing your tormented body
into the wet clay
you have dug from the cold earth
you express the only part of you
barely alive.
Your hands beat against
the clay which
Rodin kept you from
making your song.
He cannot stop you
now as you work
into a frenzy.
No mentor with a beard,
no newborn to hold,
just this wet, cold clay
you will help bring into the world.
Express the sacred part of you, Camille,
in the cold asylum
without a chisel or mallet
to free yourself.

Tom Wolfe (the prolific carver)

———— ∞ ————

Faces manifest in wood
as Tom coaxes them
into this worldly plane
calling each by their true names,
reflective of who they will be
in this life.
Tom Wolfe and the wood
join forces outside of the forest.
Chips fall into his clothes,
raining on the floor
as he whittles his companions
one by one.
They come willingly, seemingly mute.
Wizards, honey bears, fishermen, soldiers,
determined women, Santas,
house spirits, holy men, real dolls,
hound dogs and hillbillies
share their secret histories
with Tom and the people
who take them home.

Two People

———— ∞ ————

He liked Sinatra
and Artie Shaw's clarinet.
He drank cold Bud out of a can.
He ate sliced green peppers
before dinner at six.
He surrounded himself with flowers
in coffee cans and terra cotta pots.
He lives on a mountain with Sheena,
a big golden who drinks beer, too.

She liked Nat Cole
and Jerry Vale's singing.
She drank chilled vodka after golf.
She ate salted celery
before dinner at six.
She surrounded herself with needlepoint
on furniture and walls.
She lives by the beach with Dick,
her best friend who plays golf with her, too.

These two have one thing in common:
They made me.

October 12th

———— ∞ ————

On campus
a girl
lost out
at a
frat party.
The boys
without thought
brutally raped
the girl
for sport.
When they
finished raping
the girl,
they left
her behind,
believing she
was dead.
I think
of her
each day
and wonder
how she
was chosen
and wonder
how she

is doing.
I have
no answers
for myself
or her.
I only
know the
boys who
did this
are animals.
We will
not be
silent victims.
When you
violated her,
you crossed
the line
of tolerance
in Boone.
We are
angry, empowered
women asking
for justice
for all.

Bass Lake

———— ∞ ————

Water lulls
the frigid
stillness.
Light catches
the blue
swells.
Winter coolness
braces the
China expressiveness
of the lake,
the first lady
of Blowing Rock,
North Carolina.

Missing You

——— ∞ ———

At the typewriter
I freeze over
the keys.
You are responsible
for making a poet
and then I realize
you are not to be
thought of any more.
You are a dream
and a nightmare.
I still fight myself
when I want to run to
the telephone or
write you a letter.
You closed the avenue to you.
as if to punish me for
not staying within the
boundaries you set
for me.
But this was your mistake
for thinking I would
behave like a pet or
a good little woman.
This is what my struggle
with everyone

in my life is about.
I refuse to fall in line
for you or for them.
I take back my misplaced power,
never to allow another
to take the reigns of my life again.
Surrender, you say?
Surrender, I say to the God of my own understanding.
Yes, you opened a poet
and a woman to bloom and rot.
Here is my paper.
Here is my ink.
Here is my life without you in it.
The writing comes
to the page
and the loneliness
fades in the telling.

The Fighter

———— ∞ ————

for Hazel & Joan

She will not
allow the attendants
to move her around
the hospital room.
With her broken hip
she would rather crawl
around than be treated
like an infant or a non-entity
in a culture where the elderly
are treated like food which turned with age
Every waking moment,
every sleeping moment,
she fights osteoporosis,
cancer, irregular heartbeats,
lung disease and fatigue.
She fights with a sharpened mind
and a deep-rooted Episcopal truth.
I'm still here for some reason
she says, battling the foes of mortals.
Discouraged, she turns over and fights
some more I'm not ready, yet. Not yet.
I'm here. I know who I am. I know the year
and can remember every event of my life.

Don't look away when I'm talking to you.
Damn it! I'm still here and as long as I'm
here, you'll respect my way of living.
I'm not a sack of potatoes for you to carry.
I'm a person with feelings. It's not time
to pull the sheet over my face. I want to see
where I've been and I want to see where I'm going
Determined, she stays put like the tree for which
she was named
Hazel
until her first-born daughter comes.
Then Hazel will move without a word.

The Road to Linville

The mountains rise across
the blue horizon.
I see the hulking,
slate, gunpowder earth.
On the road to Linville,
Banner Elk, and Beech Mountain
the Grandfather stands over all.
White, frost bitten trees
watch over
the cathedral in Winter.
Holy ground
keeps the tongue stilled,
though the breath comes out frosted
as a cloud in transit.
I whisper goodnight
to the mountain,
a prayer
for all to be right
in the world.

Waiting by the Phone

——————— ∞ ———————

Cry a little.
Get back to work
or go look for work
like a real person.
Just get out.
Don't wait for a phone call
to keep company with you.
It's all fake.
Fiberoptics my foot.
Words are cheap to a writer.
Until they come to paper
and even then we ask
ourselves Is this for real?
Go into town.
Find a person.
Look into their eyes
and if you can,
look deeper.
And if you dare,
give them some
conversation to
chew on.

The Mystery

———— ⚮ ————

I don't know what the answer is.
I can say I love you
and the next minute
I want nothing to do with you,
because I know who you are at the base,
but you know who I am, too.
Get it right this incarnation.
There's no need for hesitation.
You already know what you're going to do.

I don't know how it will all turn out.
I can say I'm here for you
and the next minute
I'll be on my way,
because I know that this chase
is only making me blue.
Get it right this incarnation.
There's no need for hesitation.
You already know what you're going to do.

At the PO

In Blowing Rock,
people old and young
come to town
for mail
and a little socializing
at the PO
where you
know each
postmaster
by name.
There's no glass barrier
between you and your neighbor
and money is freely exchanged
for a link to the outside,
if there is
such a place.
The PO
is the center,
the hub
of this picture
post card
town
where
residents
say,

How are you?
and mean each syllable.
In Blowing Rock,
you are real
and remembered,
not lost in a tangled
metropolis.
Before moving on,
stop by the PO
and take a breath of real life.

From Germany

————— ∞ —————

Across the ocean
a soothing voice
lulls me
into a safety net
of feeling
more than
friendship.
So we play
at swords
with words,
taking chances.
Parry.
Back to
our respective
sides of the world
when the match ends.

Living in Boone

There is a man
in Boone who
is an artist
with hair,
clay,
hammers,
and paint.
Above all,
he follows
in the footsteps
of another
carpenter
whom he
loves very deeply.
In his own way,
he looks like Jesus,
so when
you break
bread and listen
to him, you imagine
the masses on the Mount
and smile
because he reminds
you of the beauty
in simplicity.

Christmas Lights

———— ∞ ————

Before Thanksgiving
white lights and red bows
adorn Main Street.
Nut brown wicker deer
sit on the lawn of the town hall
and wink at children in passing.
Joseph, Mary, and Baby
live in the silent heart of town.
In the rush,
do we remember them?
In the rush,
do we feel the love waiting for us?
Come in from the cold.
Renew the Holy One
within
each
and all.

Angels on the Walls

———— ∞ ————

Under the
embroidery
in primary colored yarns
a child sleeps
beneath angels' prayers.
Nothing enters
the room to harm
the child or the mother's
handiwork on white linen.
The prayers
stay with the child
as do the angels
themselves
as they assist
in the journey
of growing up.

Letters to a Young Poet

———— ∞ ————

Ranier Maria Rilke,
you wrote letters
to Franz Kappus,
a young poet.
Did you know
you wrote to all
of us who suffer
from this affliction
of going into ourselves
because we know
no other way of
stilling the flood waters
and living a conventional life.
You say we must be
solitary and courageous?
Some days it is hard to be brave.
We asked if we traveled
the right road,
when we shouldn't
ask such questions
for is not God leading us?
When we see another artist,
should we not encourage
them to take up the pen or brush?
We are not alone

in creating;
we are becoming
more in touch
with the Holy Ones
as you were and are.

The Street Prophet

———— ∞ ————

A man wearing
the colors
of the covenant
speaks the words
of the prophets.
He preaches on
streets, in stores,
over the din
of self-interest.
Babylon takes
little interest
in the Baptist
who weaves to live
and lives to weave
a new robe
for the Second Coming
of the King of Kings.

In Love With

———— ∞ ————

Being with you
is being in love
with the wind.
I never know when you
will tear through my life
or caress my face
in the night
or know where
you will travel without me
by your side.
You rush away so quickly.
I can never keep up with you.
But like the wind,
you return to the same places
eventually.

Thawing Out

———— ∞ ————

The snow
blows across
the green grass.
I watch the majesty
of something
greater than myself,
something older,
more powerful,
more beautiful.
The temperature
rises above normal
melting the snow
into water.
I learn from nature,
my teacher,
to wait for
the next turn
of events
in the wheel.

The Reality of Empty Pockets

She knows
nothing more
than she has seen
on the mountain.
She struggles
to keep a baby girl
in Wal*Mart specials
while she works
at the textile plant
until it closes after
Christmas. Her job
traveled South
to a warmer place.
She strains to
find a job in fine print—
one with hours agreeable
to a baby-sitter.
Somewhere
on the floor
of her 1983 Ford
lies a chewed up
Reba tape
with a message
from the outside
on it.

She can't stop
long enough
to listen.
It takes
everything
to keep the family
together.
She'd like to live up
to the Biblical Women—
if she only had the time
to read the Word.
The only words she hears
is unemployment,
honey,
and Mama.

Inner Mother

———— ∞ ————

No longer
looking outside
for acceptance—
knowing I am
the mother
of my inner
self-revelation?
If I go
hungry
it is
my doing.
If I don't
rest
it is
my fault.
When I Create
it is
my blessing.

Mary, Our Mother

——— ∞ ———

Dear Mary, Mother of God,
find us in the empty stable.
We have lost our way and cannot be whole
Without the love of our Mother, too.
Together, you and the Father
made the Son of Spirit and Flesh.
Until we believe in the unseen
more than the seen,
you will appear at farms, in caves, anywhere
the faithful will follow.
Hold us Mother.
You and the father have not left home.
We have.
Come to us, Mother. We set a place for you at the table.
Let us wait on you.
Amen.

Heather & Holly

———— ∞ ————

In the house
traces of
heather and holly
arrange them
in blue mountain pottery.
One place,
a sacred space,
fills itself with
books and papers?
scattered to the
four corners.
Without being seen
their scent
takes away mutable time.
Evergreen,
small and pink blossom,
hearty and scarlet berry,
held in memory's embrace.

The Violin

───────── ∞ ─────────

She is beautiful to him,
I've heard,
when she plays the violin.
She plays not with a bow.
but plays with all the fibers
he fell in love with
so many years ago
when they were green lovers
in the valley below.
The music finds him,
no matter how far away
he goes.
He can't resist the familiar sounds
after all this time.
She waits for him by the fire
and plays for herself in the orange glow.
Restless, he falls into
the evening, more harmonic
with her strings
than all the others
pulling him from her.

Beneath the Quilt

———— ∞ ————

He remains with her
long after he left her
standing behind a closed door.
She returns to bed with sleep
on her mind. There is no peace
after seeing him. As soon as she
puts her love away, he stands in the doorway
and pulls her into the whirlpool
she loves and dreads.
A decision turns into
indecision. She kicks the covers
off. When she reaches for them,
she smells his scent…
the only proof of him
having loved her…
until a baby comes
in summer.

Winter Burial

———— ∞ ————

Let the old issues
be buried
beneath the cold stuff.
Let the wind
cover them
in a flash
of white darkness.
Leave them
without a marker
to remember
them by.

Release

———— ∞ ————

The woman
chose a path
of briars and stones.
Broken dreams,
broken bottles
litter the ground.
Each step
brings pain and joy.
Hold on.
Hold on, she tells herself.
Then she stops.
No. No. No.
Let it go, she says.
Lighter, the woman
moves on.

The Message

———— ∞ ————

On the window
it was written,
I love Jesus.
as a protest
to the angel proclamation
Be an angel. Practice
random acts of kindness.
Did angels
not serve Jesus
in the wilderness?
Do angels
not minister
now?
If you are not open
to them,
you will not know them.

Wolves & Angels

———— ∞ ————

Meeting beneath
the pines
brushed with snow,
an angel disguised
stays close to
a hungry wolf.
She offers him
food of the spirit.
He follows the angel
to the clearing and
takes the food
from her hands.
She says nothing
before parting.
She waves and
he has already
blended with the forest.

The Palette

———— ∞ ————

The colorless wash
of lies
dries up on the palette.
A fresh brush
waits to be unwrapped
and dipped
in new colors
from untouched tubes.

Last November

On a warm pavement
we three sat
as we dined from
white paper sacks
from the heart
of Wink, Texas.
We give thanks
to have come so
far away from
the unopened pain
in our lives.
This year
we have all moved away
from our former selves,
forced to make choices
we denied the year before.
Over a plate of beans
and salsa we were
children unaware.

The Calling

Come to me, love.
Hear my voice call to you
in the night
when you rise
with the birds
before dawn.
Know I'm alive
and warm
miles away from
our mutual seduction
society.
Answer my call, love.
Then I can fall
asleep and dream
of happy endings.

The Triangle

———— ∞ ————

Mrs. Norman
entered
Georgia's
birthing room
one day.
Alfred welcomed
her warmth
into his
Eden.
Georgia painted
bones and flowers
upon a separate
desert canvas.
In one image
Mrs. Norman
took the
place
where Georgia
posed
hundreds of times.
She learned
to take
images of
Alfred,
the master

photographer.
The end
remains
to be seen
on museum walls.
Georgia embraced
her muse,
not Mrs. Norman.
No blissful,
egg shell haven
for the trio
rolled down
from divine love.
One pulls
the other
away from the other.
Only art survives.

No More

———— ∞ ————

Bundled
treasures
given
away
eyesores
a
deep
heart sore
out
of
her
mind
forever.

Desert Emotion

The moon rose
and set upon your face.
I, the fool,
believed you loved me
in the truth of morning.
You sent pretty words to my door;
you spoke them there.
Georgia dies slowly.
The bones burn black.
The red poppy bleeds.
Paper fragments
ask the question
Stieglitz?
Why take all sanity
from women supreme?
We gave love.
In offering
we are alike.
Some escape,
while some of us
splinter.

Elizabeth

———— ∞ ————

for Edward

Elizabeth
stands tall
in the quiet night,
saying more
with spirited eyes
than in
all the
compositions
left undone.

The Pinnacle

———— ∞ ————

Musicians come
to Edward
as do
old instruments
in frayed cases
needy for
taping.
He gives
them space
to create
and trade
notes
off the cuff.

Farewell

In the mist
I can see the rolling mountains
all the way into Virginia
until there is nothing
left of myself.
I wish the wind
blowing this way
a merry journey.
Could I come with you?
The answer
reverberates.
Leave my mountain…
I go without
truly leaving.

Trinity

The Young Pianist

———— ∞ ————

Over the keys
your hands
flew in
a symphony
just for you.
Sunlight lit
your smooth
back
as you played
our souls
for the
audience
one Sunday's
walk
beside
the Tennessee River.
As we watched
the glory
of your union
you pulled us
closer to
infinity.

Domestic Dreams

———— ∞ ————

Making vegetable stew
in the kitchen
I peel potatoes
for a stew
and in the heat
I carve a face
in the soft white flesh
of a spud.
For a second
I believe I am a stone cutter
or wood carver
until I slice the expressive face
into a pot
of boiling water.

Breaking Bread

———— ∞ ————

We two
break bread
and speak
openly
to cleanse
the wounds
between us
with yogurt
and humus dips
in ceramic bowls.
We resume
reflecting
eye to eye—
sisters at last.

Awakenings

——————— ∞ ———————

Etowah memories
pull the young kings
into grassy
burial mounds
stirring ancient
ancestors from
dry-eyed slumbers.
The power lies
comatose,
untapped
until
the calling
from the heart is necessity
breaks into
a multitude
of sorrowful joys.

Book

————— ∞ —————

I will end up
like so many
on the bargain table.
Marked down.
Cast aside.
A remainder
of my former glory days
faced out.

The Human Race

————— ∞ —————

From the earth
we came
when God
determined
we would be
forever
reborn.
Clay,
Spirit,
Fire,
and Water
mixed into
an explosive
entity.

Legend Tina Turner

———— ∞ ————

A woman
walks by.
A girl
from Tennessee.
picking cotton
and strawberry fruit
on hot days.
The earth
burns hot
against the skin.
She raises
her voice
to God.
Love showers
her like the stars.
A woman walks by
at home with herself.

Once More

———— ∞ ————

Writing again
resumes an act of faith
rooted in weary waiting
for acceptance
in work
of self
buried beneath
useless masks
not fitting
a new face
turned away
from passing
fruitless years.

Tornado Watch

———— ∞ ————

In the fury
of the storm
I wait quietly
taking shelter
with God
in the ditch
beside the road

Lilith, the first woman or Eve's Song

———— ∞ ————

Women
are not taught
about your days
in Eden.
You came
from the earth
like Adam,
refusing to be lorded over
by your husband.
Turning your back
upon paradise,
your spirit opened wider.
Better to be shunned
by all than to carry
the burden of Eve's curse.

The First Step

———— ∞ ————

for Julie

Courage
arrives
in
the
nick of time
to catch
a lone explorer
taking
one small step
through
the
uncharted country.
Go forward
at your own speed.
You
know
in
the
heart of understanding
where
you will land.

Resurrection

———— ∞ ————

Winter 1996

Margaret Mitchell's
writing place
rose from
smoke and ashes
on the third day.
Undefeated the
Southern Daughter resides
out of time
in the skyscraper city
of many shades.

Wandering Daughter

———— ∞ ————

Having run
and returned to point A
I find myself
running through myself
during the day
and
during the night
unsure of purpose,
design, or destiny.
It is harder
to run inside
than to jump
in the driver's seat.

Pigeon Bread

———— ∞ ————

Frantic feasting
on Haywood Street
commences
over the hard fought bounty
heaped on by a bird woman
spooning last night's cornbread
into stone wounds.
She leaves them life:
the empty remains
of someone's wife.

In the Winery

———— ∞ ————

Bold new sensations
free my spirit to know there is more
outside the plateau.
Uncork the bottle.
Smell the bouquet
Roll the wine
on the back of the tongue.
Drink to obliterate.

His Story

— ∞ —

Robert Lee Chaplin?
I never knew you in life.
A plaque on Wall Street
bares your testament
for those who stop to read.
Gentle spirit, sweep
the stars from the curb
residue of time and space:
1931-1988.
I see your truth
if not your smile
lingering in doorways.
Tell me all you know
beneath the spreading of the leaves.
I will listen.

Shoot for the moon...
even if you miss it you will land among the stars

———— ∞ ————

On a trail of stardust
wandering in search of
a paradise too complete
for my understanding
the completeness of me,
the wholeness of you,
unknown equations
waiting to be asked
into the here and now.
Wonder when your eyes will touch
my heart and invite
implosion upon itself,
flowering wildly,
entangled undergrowth
longing to be born.

Perspective

New
again.
Green.
Pushing
through
the
earth.
Warming
in
the
sun.
Taking
on
the
rain.
Slowly
blooming.
Being
all.

Two

———— ∞ ————

for Pamela

Reflective teacher
leading me back
to myself
two pieces
fitting together
forming a
bridge of
continuum
between a ram
and a bull
in a field
of tall green grass
where neither
can be seen
from the outside
looking inward
from the
Absolute

Jennifer of Asheville

———— ∞ ————

A woman
with clear insight
whispered,
The homeless
are the happiest people
I know.
No unseen weight
or industrial fears
burden them.
They just go along
the path
to glory.

Cruising on Seventy

——— ∞ ———

Two lovers
rejected by one and the same
cruise down the highway
with Alanis' angry, white woman music.
Singing out of control
the women
bond at sunset
drunk with the night,
but more sober at dawn.

Seed

———— ∞ ————

Gather the flowers in Spring.
Forget not to spread the dried seeds
on the bare, untouched earth.
Watch the birds
float
      down
           from
Heaven's respite
and remember perfection
in every movement and
every stillness.

At 914

———— ∞ ————

Opening the door
to a Southern home
designed by fragmented
family treasures
left to the living guardians
by persons long gone
a welcome face,
appears in the window
when I escape the approaching storm.

S's Perspective

———— ∞ ————

Two African-American youths
came out of the movie theater.
One man asked, Why should I
care about that movie?
It's not about my people or my time.
The other man stopped. He touched
the deepest part of meaning.
Oppression knows no one people.

Another man in a business suit
expresses violence and nudity
have no place as entertainment.
A child of Germany
cries out for the victims
in her own family
who served, fell, and lost
their bloom in Russia.

A Holocaust survivor remembers all
as if it were today.
He doesn't need to see
Hollywood's version.

A woman embraces
the American soldier
who released her
fifty summers ago.

Trinity

A director in the dark knows
that he and his children
would have been
on the other side
of the barbed wire
in another time
and Fatherland.

Wet Pavement

———— ∞ ————

She never walked through Asheville
after a rain.
It is not God's tears,
but her own
wetting the pavement
where she met him.

As for Popular Opinion

———— ∞ ————

Listen
to
the
still
waters
within,
not
to
the chatter
in the marsh.

America

———— ∞ ————

One day
the colors
will flow
like the tides,
becoming a sacred blend
of not one
or the other
in the land
of Good and Plenty.
The differences
are nowhere
but in the tiger mind
crouching low,
thriving on fears
founded on
flypaper ideas
we keep
for years.

Picnic

Women,
fear not.
We are
a realm
of probability.
Study, write, learn.
Concentrate
on worth,
not what you earn.
Keep a dream.
Spread it out
like a quilt
of your own design.
Smooth out
the bumps
and rumpled places.
Make a place
for yourself
and look up
at the sky.

Out Cold

———— ∞ ————

My chin
hit the floor and
I saw the blood
flowing out
upon coming out of the dark.
Who's blood is that?
Oh, it's mine…
was my first thought.
They flipped me over
like plywood or some
freshly caught salmon.
She'll need some stitches.
They didn't think I was listening,
but writers never stop
even after they're dead.
I spoke to the people
who tended my body.
The medics came
and I told them a story
all the way to the hospital.
I felt myself slipping out.
They brought me back
and stabilized me,
but I've never been stable.
(Thank God.)

Now here

———— ∞ ————

Now here
I am
unclear
as to
the outcome
swimming
in the
nightmare's
afterglow.
Meditation
restores
a breath of life,
bringing a
sad child
out of
nowhere.

Ferne

———— ∞ ————

Resting in the woods,
beneath the shade
of a great tree,
a fern takes root
in the rocky soil,
content to be
divine expression
on the path.
Without flowers
or scents
to woo the traveler,
the fern pushes upward.
Pacific leaves
speak to the heart
which has turned over
like a stone.

Less Words

───── ∞ ─────

Words come softly
through the
window of memory
like a goldfinch
only to fly away
in the face of reality.
I wonder how you dare
to come again
as if nothing
were said before
which maimed
a lonely heart
in a feathered breast.

Faded Glory

———— ∽ ————

for Julie

Tired, worn leather shoes
have been my constant
companions as I explored
The inner and outer reaches
of who I truly am.
They belong not in the bin.
I listen to them tell the story
of my impressions of the
people and places which
I've drawn into my private journey.
When I place them on my feet I laugh
At the gaping holes
My toes peak through
And I am reminded
Of how far I've come
And how much further
I've yet to travel.

Prairie Dance

———— ∞ ————

In the lateness of the hour
my rodeo lover watches
over me while I sleep.
It is being in the womb
all over again.
His breath becomes mine
as we are wed
Beneath an open sky.
he calls to me in such a way—
I can't help but follow
him across the lulling sea
of prairie grass.
He knows the trail
and takes me with him,
His hand clasped with mine.
The music of life begins
this dance between
Two as one.
I am breathless in his arms.

Upon Reflection

———— ∞ ————

You are asleep beside me
As you rest
I cannot love you less
I dare not love you more
You are of me
And not of me
At the same point in time.
Is this not a dream
Awakened by the soft moan
Of the wind,
Your friend from the plains
Who followed you here
And will not let you alone
- all the while leading
you back to the place
you left when you wandered
away from your home.
When your eyes engaged mine
I knew you were a man of God?
You say this may not be the end.
I say this may be the beginning.
So we stand face to face
And I wonder if we know
What the rest of this dance may be.

The Mines Children

——————— ∞ ———————

Ashley
You are light
Streaming across fiery field and ocean.
Little girl, you have the potential for greatness.
Will you ever awaken from this world's dream
and realize the seeds God's planted within
your creative soul?

Laurel
You are promise
And strength in the night
for weeping souls.
Young woman, you have wisdom
and truth as your guides.

Matthew
You are a marvelous man
hiding behind your father.
The shadows fade as your wit
ignites the hypocrisy
around you
setting the stage for change.

Sarah
You are beauty
in flower for those who stop along the way.

What does anyone know of you?
You carry the secrets of the family
In your open heart.
you are love, darling.

Kathy

———— ∞ ————

Her strength
lies behind
black eyes
determined to see
through any given
situation.

The Harvest

———— ∞ ————

The corn in the husk
Are lain gingerly in the brown grass
Awaiting the glistening mouths and eyes
Of the holy innocents.
The hands of the children
Let go of the kernels
Lost in the shaft of adulthood.

Little Bear

———— ∞ ————

Sitting in her room
You are with her.
The part of me unexpressed sits
Beside you both
On cold moonblind nights
When her mother looks away.
Only for a moment
You are my tear-stained eyes
Watching over a borrowed angel.

Burial

——— ∞ ———

Into the earth
we must go
at the unnamed hour.
How many times do thoughts
push its way into
a cluttered mind?
Mortality?
Eternity?
A rest away from this battle
called life.

As for Joanna's Passing

Angel wings poised for flight
of a soul ready to leave
The earthbound school
For higher aspirations
and a little restful contemplation,
tested the winds
at Easter time
and left us to ponder
the universe alone.

Trinity Church

———— ∞ ————

I climbed the tower
all alone
and found nothing
but the dusty, vacant rooms
of the past.
I refused to clean them
and kept climbing to the top.
Once by a window I peered into the garden below.
Almost falling
to my great joy
I pulled myself
back inside so the climb could resume.
The light flooded me as I reached the top,
coming out of the dimly lit rooms
into God's arms.

The Anointed One

———— ∞ ————

A girl child
clutching a small, cloth Easter bunny
in her arms
came to the table of Christ.
I could see the love
between the two of them
and it reached into
my own heart.
I, too, had been
in her place
and am in her place
in this flicker in time.

Kneeling Before St. Mary

In Monsignor's
Holy Church
Mary stands in a blue light
As two angels
Kneel by her feet.
She comforts me
When no one else can.
Mary is warm, not cold to the touch.
She answers the faithful.
Even when the desired outcome
Doesn't happen the way
We would like it to.

Embraced

If I could hold your face
in my hands
I would speak words of love
or I might just hold you silently.
Was it the priest or the man
who swept me into
the fire?
Will you stir the embers
or allow them to fade and die?
If there is no trace
no one can say a word.
You are the cross I bear.
I am the rose you plucked
from the bush.

The Sacrament

———— ∽ ————

Father wept.
He rubs his gentle eyes
before communion.
He visited the morgue
the night before
as priests sometimes do.
Behind closed doors
he questions the reasoning
of plucking one so young
from the parish.
He'll say the right words
at the proper time.
He can offer no explanation
to the parents
or to himself.
He sighs and resumes
a walk in faith.

Twice Kissed

———— ∞ ————

With you I am twice kissed
for it is not just these lips
you brush with your own.
Our souls mesh
until we cannot tell
one from another.
When I first heard your name,
I paused between breaths.
When I first saw you,
I saw myself.
When you have healed me,
I have offered you no less.

Prayers for Umfúndisi

———— ∞ ————

From his children

In the sea
of worshipers
he stands alone…
shuffling a sermon,
eyeing the pews
for a number
known only to God.
Above the Trinity
Umfúndisi is fire.
The double-edged sword
of truth hangs over him.
The eldest girl holds fast to
Father Daddy's robes.
The middle daughter pirouettes around them.
The baby son draws in the dirt beside his feet.
They go with him
even though they are left behind
to watch the nighttime showers
from their beds.

Sweet Jesus,
watch over the trail of the comet.
Amen.

The Wifely Garden

———— ∞ ————

A flower desires water,
light, and a place to grow.
This woman is God's daughter
deserving the same tender love you sow
in the giving of the rings you bought her
so many years ago.

Tíxo

———— ∞ ————

Upon Christ's altar
the feast is prepared.
An Afrikán hymn surrounds us
as does His love.
It is this way?
the old way? in the small chapel
beneath the great church.
Each move the cannon makes
represents another face which
the fast moving congregation
neglects to pause for.
They look not into the eyes
of the man sent by the Christ
out of Afriká
to the mountain town,
nor do they embrace dusk's angels
until Umfúndisi stands near.
We must unlearn the false teachings of this world,
choosing to stay awake
without rolling into slumber.
We do so one by one
as the bread breaks
and the chalice passes
across the family table.

Pondering In King David's Hot Tub

——— ∞ ———

Preacher-Poet?
Don't you know it?
I'm certain your life will change.
It's not so strange
to rearrange
the furniture of life.
Just don't blow it!

Trish's Dream

———— ∞ ————

Between two men on a nightmare run,
you are not stopping long enough
to hear your inner voice.
Fate stirs you
out of the deepest slumber
to rise and face the morning.

Lon D.

—————— ∞ ——————

My friend
looks over his shoulder.
He laughs from the gut,
living with a wisdom
spun from
his grandfather's bough.
He is the panther
lashing his tail
at the white moon.
He is the gentle
and proud Inkòsikazi.

Just Next Door

My neighbor's children
Play piano
On summer afternoons
Their mother doesn't realize
I take a wild delight
Being within earshot
As I share their lives intimately
Without leaving my room.

Apache Rose

———— ∞ ————

Of your father's spirit
and your mother's song
you rose from the deserts
ancient wisdom.
Daughter, you are kissed
by the great spirit.
So peacefully asleep
in your mother's sweet arms
you dream of destiny
on the path as healer and holy woman
tending to those who have lost themselves.
They will call you blessed
Apache Rose—
a flower in the wilderness of the soul.
Welcome.

Lit

——— ∞ ———

for Sherri Lynn (Lady Godiva) Clark

Beauteous keeper of the gate,
guard your spiritual box
from those who would turn
it upside down.
Songs will come
on the wings of angels.
They are yours
to gather
from the night skies.
Listen.

Thia

———— ∞ ————

Not
restricted
by time and space
you know you are home
anywhere.
Stay
on the path
to self-discovery,
loving all
of Thia.

Julia's Ashes

Four blackened chimneys
Rise to the sky.
My being stands at half-mast.
My charred heart cries.
The children look upon
The tired battle
Between their parents.
Another chapter
Winds down,
Written in soot and tears.

The Barefoot Angel and the Evangelist

———— ∞ ————

Nowhere else
does the angelic boy
wish to be
other than in the safe arms
of his earthly father.

Nothing else
does the angelic boy
wish to see
other than the laughing eyes
of his earthly father.

In this moment
father and son
find Heaven
not outside of themselves
but within
their hearts.

His Life Is This Room

———— ∞ ————

The Canon charges through hollow halls
as if he were the king of all.
Open books, strewn lives,
and mad dashes on paper
litter his stone walled sanctuary.
A few crayon pictures
tacked upon the open door
console the man behind
the pontifex
when no one else can.

Angel Tears

Angel Tears

———— ∞ ————

In the wild garden
of Trinity Church,
broken bricks surround
the contemplative one
with weeds overgrown
and the flowers dried.
The studying goes on,
relentless seeker.
The Canon looks into books.
The Angel looks into human hearts.

Through the hall
I travel timelessly
with my head covered in ceaseless prayers
and midnight reflection.

Father, forgive me.
I know not why
I've come to you.
Before your door
I tremble.

My wax wings curl up
and melt into a pool
at my feet?
So close to the sun
my feathers are useless.

Ashes & Embers

Laugh at the woman
humbled by you.

Christmas is coming.
The tree is alive in light.
The babe,
the man,
and the Son
of the only God
hold your sweet three.
They are more precious
than anyone or anything
in this challenging life.

I'm a persistent angel.
God knew I could handle you.
No one else dares tell you the truth?
except the spirit of your mother.
I will listen even when you ignore me
and curse at me for coming through the red doors.
I see all sides of you?
the beautiful, the ugly.
All is good, Father.
You know this in the deepest part of yourself.

In your heart, know this?
no matter if the whole world
turns away from you,
I will be here.

If you denied my existence, what then?
I would have to look into my heart,
forgiving you as I have myself
for all transgressions.

A Long Time Coming

———— ∞ ————

Zoë and Rhonda
Flow to one another
As the flood of tears
Brings them closer
To being daughter and mother.

The Gift

———— ∞ ————

Dearest Soul:
In all creation,
you are more perfect
than you know.
I praise the strength
forged by pain,
hammered by will,
yet saved by love.
Others cannot
carry your dreams.
Teach the blessed three
closest to you.
They would become
lost in the cold sea
without your loving reassurance
telling your three babies
that it's right to be true to their dreams.
As you teach them
recall your personal mission.
Resume life and still the outside voices
tearing at the soft-knowing self.
Love,
the Spirit

Passing Through

———— ∞ ————

for Wendy

As you travel to your heart,
remember to gaze
at marmalade sunsets.
Smile with the joy
of how you've made
a difference
in other people's lives.
For this is how
I'll remember you.

Jeni

———— ∞ ————

Tearing through
the dark as a celestial force,
you are forcefully brilliant.
Be nothing less
than you know
you are capable of being.
Change the unchangeable.
Think the unthinkable.
Know that you know, cool mama.
There ain't nobody
brighter than you.

Renewal

Advent I

As I looked across my blue hymnal
A golden child looked into
My tired heart
And once again
I soared above my own
Broken pieces.

Advent II

I saw the music run through him
As it did me.
The joy on his face
Outshone the stars.
For once he looked happy
Without the weight of the past year
In his eyes.

Advent III

Healing,
The touch of Christ
Pulled at my heart
Shattering the ice queen
On the streets.

Advent IV

No children.
No wife.
Keeping the faith until their return,
I warm my hands with the homeless
In the basement below.

Love Shattered

———— ∞ ————

I look into his dark black pearl eyes
And Lord Jesus I am lost, forever lost in him and me.
My lips long to kiss him in the night.
My dreams echo memories of his soul drawn upon
     mine.
He's so close and he'll never know how much I love him.
He cannot fathom one so young having feelings so old.

Mr. & Mrs.

———— ∞ ————

Turning the pages of music
soaring above all else
this man and wife
are content to work
side by side,
notes themselves in
love's crescendo.

On the Spiritual Slopes

———— ∞ ————

Behind the blue veil
he saw me as the spiritual interloper
in a traditional house of the Lord.
He spoke to me in silence
Each time he made another pass
around the mountain.

Dual Confession

———— ∞ ————

We came to an understanding
on a sunny day beneath leafless trees.
He is my spiritual father, now,
and I am his friend.
We see the pain buried in layers.
We unravel them like a life shroud,
looking at them in the light without shame.

Handyman

———— ∞ ————

Sees all.
Knows all.
Says nothing,
but the gospel truth
about all the fancy ladies
fighting nail and tooth.

A Mother's Vigil

———— ∞ ————

Southern woman of grace and steel
knowing who is false and real.
Ministering on her own,
until her precious daughter has flown.

My Bishop will King you with Jesus

———— ∞ ————

On a chess board,
quietly bowing before God,
I look into the Bishop's face
as he whispers,
If you truly love him,
you will hand him back to me.
Merely a 'Christmas Knight,"
I obey.

Tennessee Woman

——— ∞ ———

From the beginning,
you have placed the seeds of destruction on my plate,
thinking you could make me eat pomegranate
and send my soul to Hades.
Any harm you've caused
will come to you tenfold
not by my hand, but your own.

A Pearl Before Swine

———— ∞ ————

Holy, Holy, Holy God,
the frightened people
threw away
the gift sent
last Easter morning
to the big church.
Scripture wrote itself
out every Sunday coffee hour.
The pearl fell between the pews.
It still gleams brightly
on the dark, wooden floor.

Ladies Agreement

In the pulpit,
the pious priest speaks of sins,
not of his own blackened heart
or of the women
who hide his indiscretions
with lies and sweet laughter.

A Woman's Last Stand

——— ∞ ———

In dignity
she stands on the threshold of a new life
shaking out the old one
in the backyard.
The dust sticks in her throat a little.
She's determined to clean house
before the day ends.
Slowly, deliberately,
she rolls the family colors up
for the move east.

Cast Out

———— ∞ ————

Alone,
I am priest and parishioner
at my solitary Eucharist.
Three candles are lit
in memory of the Trinity.
Their flames flicker
as I read psalm twenty-seven.
Beware, dark forces.
I am on the mend.
I'll rise above this loss of faith
and claim it as my own.

An Ex-Preacher Sums It Up For You

——— ∞ ———

The man with the backwards collar
Will have a great fall.
Selah
You know he came out of Afriká
Dressed in snowy robes.
Selah
He has no feelings
In his closed heart.
Selah
Hang in there, girl,
Because it's not done, yet.
Selah.

Asheville

———— ∞ ————

Other people find it's strange,
To go through life so unchanged.
Little do they know the error,
Of how Pope Joan stood in terror
Caused by the unknowing congregation
Of Biltmore stature and reputation.

Finis

About the Author

———— ∞ ————

Joan Noeldechen has been published in June Cotner's *Bless the Day &* *Bedside Prayers* as well as in literary journals and magazines. She is currently at work on several projects, including a collection of short stories set in North Carolina.

Printed in the United States
57369LVS00003B/64

9 780595 140787